YOU KNOW YOUR DOG LOVES YOU BECAUSE...

The Sweet, Silly, and Scientific Ways Our Dogs Show Us How Much They Love Us

D1343442

by Jeff Parks
illustrations by Mark Sean Wilson

YOU KNOW YOUR DOG LOVES YOU BECAUSE...

Printed in the United States of America
ISBN: 978-0-578-73409-5
First Printing: 2020

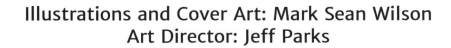

Illustrations and Cover Art: Mark Sean Wilson
Art Director: Jeff Parks

This book is dedicated to every dog out there.
You make our lives better by being the wonderful, loving
animals you are. We're lucky to have you.

Acknowledgements

The authors wish to give special thanks to
Kelly Bradymire and Donna McFarland for their support.
Both of you contributed to the success of this book with your
passion for the subject, feedback, expertise, and sunny
optimism. Thank you so much for all you did.

But First, a Little Tale

Thousands of years ago, a wolf set off from his pack looking for food. He was hungry and it was bitterly cold outside. In his journey, he happened upon a caveman cooking some meat on a small outdoor fire.

The wolf had been warned by his pack to stay away from humans or he would get rocks and other weapons thrown at him. Starving from hunger, the wolf took a chance. He got just close enough for the caveman to see him.

The wolf's stomach growled just as the caveman turned to notice him. However, instead of throwing a rock at the wolf, the caveman broke off some of the meat he was cooking and threw it near the wolf for him to eat.

After the wolf finished eating, the caveman got up and headed towards his cave. Noticing the extreme chill away from his fire, the caveman looked at the wolf and motioned for him to come sit by the fire he was now abandoning.

The wolf, knowing a good thing when he saw it, walked over to the fire's warmth, laid down, and drifted off to sleep.

When the wolf woke up that morning, he was amazed to find himself unharmed. When he told the pack of his incredible night, bonding with the human, the other wolves didn't believe him.

However, the wolf, convinced that the human wasn't a threat, found a few wolves willing to take a chance with him for easy food and a warm place to sleep at night. All they had to do was be nice in return.

Those wolves found what they were looking for and eventually evolved over the years to become the many wonderful species of dogs we know of today.

Why is this story important to our book? Because ever since dogs evolved from wolves, some people have claimed that dogs show us what we think is love, but it isn't love at all. It is really just them showing us what they think we want to see in order for them to get food and a safe place to live.

So do our dogs really love us or not? We wanted to find out the truth. So we combed over the scientific data and read countless stories from dog owners, and we found that yes, our dogs do indeed love us! As if there was ever any doubt. And our book illustrates all the different ways our dogs love us. From the scientific, to the sweet, to the silly.

Enjoy.

They're willing to try on every silly outfit you bring home and they aren't even mad about it.

After a good brushing they have gifted you a clone of themselves.

When you go to get the mail and return two minutes later, they treat you like they haven't seen you in ages.

They'll take out the trash for you.

They showed you the correct pose for downward dog.

They stare lovingly into your eyes. They are the only non-primate to use eye contact with their humans to form a special bond.

No matter how large they are, they're always willing to make space on the couch for you.

They say so much with just a head tilt. What are they saying? "I love you, but I have no idea what you want from me."

They make sure that the "dog days of summer" are the best days of summer.

They warm the bed for you.

They'll never air your dirty laundry,
but they will steal it so they can
be near your scent when you're away.

They will follow you to the ends of the earth... unless the ends of the earth is a bathtub.

They graduated school with honors.

They want you to meet their friends. Even if those friends are fleas they know from the dog next door.

They enjoy it when you rub their bellies as much as you enjoy doing it.

They are always willing to try your fast food first, just on the off chance it hasn't been cooked properly and will make you sick. One can never be too careful.

They follow you into the bathroom and never leave, no matter how awful the smell.

Your favorite song to sing along to is also their favorite.

They'll never put you in their doghouse, even after you take them to the vet.

They know it isn't truly family night until they show up.

They destroyed that "bomb" that was going to hurt their friend, and that also kept changing the Animal Planet channel to some boring, non-Animal Planet channel.

They always know just what to do to cheer you up.

They are honest with you when you smell.

Every time you throw the ball, no matter how high, how far, or how much mud they have to travel through, they always bring it back to you.

When they are very excited to see you, they pee a little. It's a scientific fact, so cut them a little slack and remember, they do it because they love you.

They like, totally get your vibe.

Their instinct is to fiercely protect you from danger...even when none exists.

They're willing to sacrifice their waistline for yours.

Even when you're away from them for a significant amount of time, they always give you a hero's welcome on your return.

They give you an excuse to use that super expensive vacuum you bought.

They warn you that there is a murderer in your front yard, no matter how many times you tell them that it's "just the mailman."

They share their baby with you. It may look like just another toy, but it is in fact their baby, and they have entrusted their baby to you.

They go after the pizza guy who they know is really the "mailman" in disguise, and is there to hurt you.

They will be your dance partner any time you want them to be.

They dig for buried treasure so you can retire.

When the storm comes,
they know there is no safer place
than to be with you.

They feel comfortable passing gas in front of you.

When you are scared to look forward,
and too ashamed to look back,
they are always right beside you, reminding you
that you have a loving friend in them.

Every morning they get you moving in the right direction.

After a long day at work, they make sure the first thing
you see when you open the door
is their happy, cheerful face.

They often defy the natural laws of physics so they can be fresh and clean for you.

Because unlike their friend, the cat,
they can't wait to come to you
after they hear you call their name.

They alert you that as adorable as that little squirrel outside looks,
they just know they're up to no good.

They're always ready to "play ball."

When you wake up on the wrong side of the bed, they are always there to remind you of how beautiful and wonderful you are.

They learn tricks and do them on your command... well, sometimes.

Whether they're certified or not, they are your therapy dog.

They know they're the perfect accessory for anything you wear.

They love your cooking.
Especially when it ends up on the floor.

Not only do they know the "good boy" or "good girl" is them, but more importantly, they know the "good human" is you.

If you loved one of our illustrations, we can personalize it for you by featuring your dog and yourself in the same illustration!

You can choose between black & white or color for your personalized illustration.

For more information contact us at: yourdoglovesyoubecause@gmail.com

Jeff Parks is an author and editor. He mostly writes about the wonderful world of dogs and cats. Jeff also operates a charity fund devoted to animal causes.

Mark Sean Wilson has been scratching his way to the top of the illustrator heap his whole life. He is fascinated with illustration and cartoons but he didn't truly go professional with his talents until he earned an associate degree in graphic design and multimedia. He has since been illustrating children's books and comics for 25 years. You can see Mark's work at: www.markerdoodle.com

Printed by Amazon Italia Logistica S.r.l.
Torrazza Piemonte (TO), Italy